HOW TO IDENTIFY A MALCONTENT BEFORE YOU MARRY HER

By

BISHOP OCHEI INNOCENT

Contents

CHAPTER ONE

LOVE VERSUS MARRIAGE

Are they the same?

These days, total strangers get acquainted and wed on the same day. They meet, to give a handy example, at a bus park and go on from there to wed, on the same day, at the marriage registry. Faster than photocopying!

There is certainly nothing wrong with love at first sight. It is something we probably cannot help. The very first day I saw my wife; I fell in love and knew I would marry her. I think it is something to do with our chemistry. The thing just connected and swept me off my feet.

I can therefore understand people falling in love at first sight. Sometimes, love comes as an irresistible tsunami sweeps off everything on its path, including commonsense and due diligence.

However, marriage is not the same thing as love. Sometimes, we even mistake a crush or infatuation for love and we all know the implications of that. But that is not my focus.

The differences between love and marriage must be identified and noted. Though they are quite many permit me to mention only a few below:

1. Marriage is something deeper. It fries longer and is not an event but a process.
2. Love is narrow. It is chemistry between two persons. Marriage goes beyond the two persons involved.

3. Love is not constrained to permanency but marriage is expected to last going by family values and societal norms. In simple language, extended relatives do not grieve much when two lovers separate compared to when a marriage crashes!
4. Marriage involves unborn children. No child would want to be born into a broken home or with sickle cell.
5. Marriage sometimes has political implications. The interests represented in the exchange of vows have to be considered seriously.
6. Marriage is often a union of two extended families. They also have some interests to protect. Therefore, the car of their enthusiasm takes long to kick start.
7. Marriage involves the health of unborn generations. Some ailments are hereditary and

children born within such
marriage inherit such defects.
8. At times, marriage involves a
fusion of two diverse cultures. So
someone has to bear the brunt of
preparing the couple for culture
shock.
9. Some marriages affect two or more
nations. They need time to
establish what is in the marriage
for them.
10.	Marriage involves a wider
circle of friends and fellow
worshippers. All of whom have to
prepare.

Should marriage therefore be
treated with levity?

"Watch and pray that you fall not into temptation..."

Mathew 26:41

CHAPTER TWO

WHO IS A MALCONTENT?

I always like the reader and me to be on the same page in all things I teach. This happens when we set out with a definition of major words found in our topic.

If you look again at the topic of this book, you will notice that the key word is **"malcontent."** What does it mean?

The Cambridge Oxford Dictionary describes it as:

**'1.   A person who is
not satisfied with the way things
are, and who complains a lot and
is unreasonable and difficult to
deal with.**

2.   <u>Unpleasant people in general</u>

Google on its part defines a malcontent as:

> **"A person who is dissatisfied
> and rebellious.
> "It was too late to stop the
> malcontents with a show of
> force"**

From the forgoing, we can safely assume that a malcontent is a person who:

1. Is unreasonable.
2. Rebellious in nature.
3. A serial complainant.

4. A difficult person to relate with.
5. Always dissatisfied.
6. Unpleasant as a result of 1-5 above.
7. One that can make life miserable for you.

Is that the type of wife or husband that you want to settle down with for life?

CHAPTER THREE

HOW TO KNOW A MALCONTENT

An African proverb says that it is not during the eating that you know a child that will rush the food. Rather, it is during the washing of hands.

Same goes for marriage. It is not during the marriage itself that your partner manifests his or her negative attitude to life. Rather, it is during the period leading up to the wedding. This time is also known as the time of courtship.

This is normally a period set aside for the two persons directly involved to come up close and study one another. It is assumed that in the process of dating and all that, the couple gets to know one another, particularly their characteristics.

Some argue that a few persons are known to pretend effectively during the entire courtship. Well, that is possible.

However, the other party should be more prayerful and could do any of two things.

1. Could go with a relation to help him or her study the other party. That was what Abraham did by sending his trusted servant with Isaac to help pick a wife amongst his own people. The observation in that case was done by the accompanying servant. This is to be recommended because they say those in love are blind.

During this period, if you want to avoid marrying a malcontent, you should watch out for the following:

1. He or she will be constantly nagging. Such a person will always find something to complain about. Because the relationship is just starting, the nagging party many not be brazen and blunt in his or her actions but they will be there. Most times, they will be as subtle as the serpent and tricky as the fox but cannot fool a keen eye.
2. Insatiability. It is hard for you to get a thank you from him or her because nothing you ever do will satisfy him or her. The demands continue to come.
3. The spirit of competition will be manifesting gently. He or she will like to move with the Joneses all the time. He or she will like to compare your coming wedding with those of others who' income may not be known to both of you.
4. Note that it is very hard to please a spend drift. Give her blank checks from time to time to see how he or she handles the test.

I once went shopping with a girl.
She picked and dropped items
from every good within sight in the
very first row of the supermarket. I
had to quickly intervene to save
the day. She did not even ask me
how much I had.
She repeated same thing on a
number of occasions.

5. Constant quarrels over material
things. Such person will not care
about your feelings at that time of
his or her madness. He or she
finds it difficult, managing their
disappointment, when you do not
meet up with their expectations.

6. The most important thing to watch
out for is pride. The peacock spirit
will make those who have it to
want to massage their egos. They
can throw away their scruples just
to do that.

7. Does he or she have fear of God?
The fear of God makes people
moderate in the things they do.
People are driven by what they
reverence. Those who fear poverty

so much can kill or do something close to that to get their way.

6.   Outlandish dressing. Watch out for people who are moderate in all things. Lifestyles cost money to maintain and trouble erupts when we are not able to maintain certain standards. If you see signs of outlandishness from day one and are not able to meet up, think twice.

7.   Pretense. This is difficult to catch off guard. However, being very watchful and paying attention to little things, enable us to detect things like this. Look out for such things when they are not expecting your look.

8.   Lying. It starts from day one. However, most times we say they are "white lies". There is nothing like white lies. A lie is a lie and a liar is a liar. Run from something you cannot curb. Most adults, especially those mature enough for marriage, have become dry woods. Any attempt to bend them a little, breaks them,

9. Watch out for the penchant to buy on credit. Such a person is likely to drain your resources.

10. Evil Association. What kind of friends and associates does he or she have? They say evil communication corrupts good manners. Such a person might come under peer pressure along the line. It is better to know the kind of pressure she or he bows to before the marriage. How she or he handles pressure is also important.

11. Talking about the company we keep. It could be a good thing to take a look at the parents of the person you want to marry. Do they have godly contentment?

12. Take a look at schools attended. Could the parents have afforded it or they just sent the child there just to massage their ego. Do not forget that an apple does not fall far from the tree. Whatever he or she might have seen the parent do, they might want to repeat in their own marriage unless there is an

intervention somewhere along the line, such as being born again.

13. What Kind of books or journals, if at all? What is written reform or destroy lives. What we read or fail to read, matters a dozen!

14. Make out time and go listen to her Pastor if any. What kind of spiritual food she is being fed matters too. Faith comes by hearing and hearing by the word of God and of course, how the word is delivered.

15. Monitor her choice television programs for the same reasons mentioned in the last five points above.

FINAL WORD

A stitch in time, they say, saves nine. Prevent what you can while you still have the time to do so.

 Do not be carried away by the wining and dining that goes with courtship.

Marriage is too serious to be handled with levity.

Never rush into it. Take time to do your home work.

Make sure you are ready for it and that you have the right person.

In management, we talk about *total quality management.* The marriage and the processes leading up to it must be of high quality. If any aspect of the arrangement is flawed, the whole thing will be affected. Do not forget that your choice forms the very foundation of your marriage and the Bible says:

Psalm 11:3 (KJV)

3 If the foundations be destroyed, what can the righteous do?

THANK YOU SO MUCH

 Should you have questions, please feel free to email the author on: newochei@gmail.com.

You can also help us by leaving a review on Amazon. This will help somebody else one way or the other.

For the author, your review will help prepare a second edition.

Thanks once more.

-BISHOP OCHEI INNOCENT

ABOUT THE AUTHOR

Bishop Ochei Innocent, 64, a trained counselor, is currently the President of New Dimension Seminaries International. He regularly teaches theology and is of the Pentecostal married to a prophetess, Elizabeth and they are blessed with four adult children.

He has been a Christian for about three decades persuasion.

OTHER BOOKS BY THE SAME AUTHOR

1. SEVEN BIBLICAL QUESTIONS MOST CHRISTIANS CANNOT ANSWER.

2. FORTY MAJOR EVANGELISM MISTAKES MOST CHURCHES MAKE

LET US PRAY

Father, I commit your son/daughter into your hand. Open their eyes to see what needs to be seen before they commit to any satanic union. Do not allow them to overlook things that can make their marriage dead on arrival.

We bind the spirits of pretense and cheating. Do not allow them to overcome us and never allow us to make costly mistakes that will ruin our destiny.

Help us to make the right decisions and
at the right time, we pray in the name of
Jesus Christ of Nazareth.

Amen.

ABOUT THE BOOK

Some things in life are preventable.

Failure in marriage is one such.

A stone coming from afar cannot burst your eye.

This book is a guide to help you identify and escape evil stones that ruin marriage even before you wed.